GEO KIDS

Exploring A FIELD

By
Holly Duhig

BookLife PUBLISHING

©2019
BookLife Publishing
King's Lynn
Norfolk PE30 4LS

Printed in Malaysia.

A catalogue record for this book is available from the British Library.

ISBN: 978-1-78637-436-3

Written by:
Holly Duhig

Edited by:
Madeline Tyler

Designed by:
Gareth Liddington

Photocredits:

Cover - MiVa, aSuruwataRi, SERGEY RYZHOV, Hapy Art, BORIS LUKIANOV, Valentina Razumova, Markus Mainka, 2 - Willem Havenaar, 4 - Patrick Foto, 5 - Patrick Foto, 6 - J. Marjis, Patrick Foto, 7 - Patrick Foto, Photographee.eu, 8 - Volodymyr Nikitenko, TheaDesign, bofotolux, 9 - Volodymyr Nikitenko, 10 - Patrick Foto, dkingsleyfish, Ruud Morijn Photographer, 11 - daksun, MNStudio, 12 - Lotus_studio, Fotoluminate LLC, 13 - Timmary, smereka, 14 - Bianca Grueneberg, THPStock, 15 - MIA Studio, 16 - Patrick Foto, Atonsov85, 17 - svrid79, Worldpics, 18 - Beata Becla, Patrick Foto, 19 - tomertu, Patrick Foto, 20 - Daniel Prudek, 21 - Patrick Foto, 22 - Patrick Foto, Anna Grigorjeva, 23 - Pressmaster.

Images are courtesy of Shutterstock.com. With thanks to Getty Images, Thinkstock Photo and iStockphoto.

CONTENTS

Words that look like **this** can be found in the glossary on page 24.

EXPLORING A FIELD

My name is Sarah and I like going camping with my family in the school holidays. Our teacher didn't give us any homework to do over the holidays; instead, we could do a project of our choice.

My project is going to be about exploring a field!

Sarah Song's Field Project

This is the field we are camping in. The grass is green and the weather is warm: it's spring!

BALL GAMES!

I'm very good at playing catch!

There are many different types of field. The one we are camping in has grass growing in it. It is perfect for playing ball games with my brother.

Grassy fields are also very good for walking dogs in. My dog is called Lola; she is still a puppy, so she has lots of energy for walks!

Groundskeeper

Grassy campsite fields have to be mowed often and taken care of by a groundskeeper.

WEEDS IN FIELDS

Stinging Nettles

Dandelion

Daisy

Stinging nettles grow in Europe, North America, northern Africa and Asia!

In grassy fields, there are often a lot of weeds and most of them grow around the edges. The field we are camping in has stinging nettles, daisies and dandelions.

Stinging nettles have tiny hook-shaped hairs on them that can sting you if you brush past them. They do this to protect themselves from being eaten by animals.

Geo-Kid Top Tip!

Stinging nettles aren't dangerous, but they can cause a painful rash.

COUNTRY WALKS!

Stile

Geo-Kid Top Tip!

Always bring plenty of water with you when you go for a long walk.

When we go camping, we go on lots of country walks. We end up seeing lots of different fields. To get from one field to another, you sometimes have to climb over a stile.

I always wear my wellies to go on country walks. There are lots of lanes to walk down alongside the fields. The tractors use these lanes to get into the fields.

Tractor Tracks

Sometimes the lanes have muddy puddles to jump in!

CROPS IN FIELDS

Oats Growing in a Field

Some fields are used to grow fruits, vegetables and grains. Farmers grow grains such as wheat, barley and oats. Grains help to make things such as cereal and biscuits.

The foods that farmers grow in fields are called crops. They harvest their crops using big machines such as combine harvesters.

Wheat contains lots of protein and is very good for you!

Combine harvesters separate the heads of wheat from the stem, and then the kernels from the head. The kernels are the part we eat!

VISITING A FARM!

The fields that horses live in are called paddocks.

Some fields are for growing crops, but some are for keeping animals. We are going to a farm where we can see lots of different animals that live in fields. My favourite animals are horses.

At this farm they let you feed the lambs with milk from a bottle. Lambs' wool is very soft.

Lots of lambs are born in the spring.

ANIMALS IN FIELDS

Here is some sheep's wool I found on the grass.

My woolly hat is made from sheep's wool that has been dyed pink.

Farmers can shear and sell a sheep's thick woolly coat. Their wool gets turned into yarn and used to make clothes.

Cows live on farms too. Here are some things I found out about cows:

* Cows live in fields in big groups called herds.
* Baby cows are called calves.
* Cows spend about eight hours a day eating!
* They like to graze on the grass in their field.

Alfalfa

Cows also like eating alfalfa.

BIKE RIDES!

I made a bouquet!

We like to go on bike rides when we are camping. We go past lots of fields full of flowers. These fields are very beautiful, and I love exploring them!

I love smelling the flowers. My brother has **hay fever** which means the flowers make him sneeze. He always takes tissues with him when we go on a bike ride.

Geo-Kid Top Tip!

Watch out for bees when smelling flowers!

FLOWERS IN FIELDS

Pollen

Some flower fields are there so that insects such as bees have something to eat and make honey with. Bees go from flower to flower drinking nectar, which they use to make honey. When they do this, they pick up the flower's powdery pollen too.

When bees fly to new flowers, they take this pollen with them. This helps the other flowers to make new seeds, which helps new flowers to grow!

When you have hay fever, it means that pollen from trees, grass and sometimes flowers can make you feel like you have a cold.

FUN IN THE FIELD!

I love exploring all of the different types of fields near our campsite! I've learnt a lot about all the plants and animals that live in them, but it's probably time for a rest now.

After all, there's one thing we haven't done yet. It's time for… a picnic!

GLOSSARY

bouquet a beautifully arranged bunch of flowers

dyed to change the colour of something using a dye

groundskeeper a person who cares for an area of land

harvest to gather crops

hay fever an allergy caused by pollen or dust which causes itchy eyes and a runny nose

kernels the edible parts of a grain

nectar a sweet liquid made by flowers in order to attract insects

protein an important nutrient that is found in foods such as meat, eggs and grains

rash a red, itchy and painful area of skin

shear to cut the wool off a sheep or other animal

INDEX